The Power of
IMPARTATION

The Need for Divine Appointments
with Spiritual Fathers

McDougal & Associates
Servants of Christ and stewards of the mysteries of God

The Power of
IMPARTATION

The Need for Divine Appointments
with Spiritual Fathers

By

Eddie T. Rogers

Original cover design by Lara York
zoecreationgrafx@bellsouth.net

Published by:

McDougal & Associates
P.O. Box 194
Greenwell Springs, LA 70739-0194
www.thepublishedword.com

McDougal & Associates is dedicated to the spreading of the Gospel of Jesus Christ to as many people as possible in the shortest time possible.

ISBN 13: 978-0-9777053-0-6
ISBN 10: 0-9777053-0-7
Printed in the United States of America
For Worldwide Distribution

DEDICATION

I have been blessed with many spiritual teachers and mentors, from whom I have received an impartation. Each one contributed a grace that I needed for that specific time. Paul wrote to the Corinthian church of the first century:

> *For even if you had ten thousand others to teach you about Christ, you have only one spiritual father.*　　　1 Corinthians 4:15, NLT

That has certainly been true for me. The Lord sent Dan Duke into my life to become that father, after the passing of my natural father. Dan has loved me through hard times, both personal and ministerial. He has been a great counselor, adviser, and, at times, added needed correction. All of those qualities make a good father.

He has never condemned me or turned his back on me, even when others did. He told me once, "God has sent me to love you through hard times, not condemn you for them." He has been to me the *"friend who sticks closer than a brother"* (Proverbs 18:24). I am eternally grateful to the Father for sending me this wonderful relationship.

Therefore, it is with much love that I dedicate this book to my friend, colleague, and spiritual father, Dr. Dan Duke.

ACKNOWLEDGMENTS

I also want to recognize the other men and women of God who have added grace upon grace to me with regards to ministry. Some of the names will be instantly recognizable. The others are known to Heaven. Most of these people I have had personal relationships with, and the others have sown invaluable spiritual growth into me through their teaching and preaching. Many of them have already graduated and finished their race. Regardless, in some way, I am indebted to them all.

They are (in alphabetical order): Rev. Mel Bond, Rev. Charles Carrin, Rev. Randy Clark, Rev. Kenneth E. Hagin, Rev. John C. Hamrick, Dr. Christian Harfouche, Rev. Ruth Ward Heflin, Dr. Rodney Howard-Browne, Rev. Bill Johnson, Rev. Franklin Rogers, Dr. Charles "Tiny" Schaus, Dr. Bob Shattles, Dr. J.T. Spinks, Dr. Charles Stanley, and Rev. Ben F. Turner. Thank you!

To my wife, Michelle Rogers, for believing in me, and for your constant encouragement and love. You are indeed another dimension of grace and mercy added to my life.

To my dear friend, Harold McDougal, for his gift of assuming the arduous task of turning a manuscript into a book. I am grateful for your time and talents.

CONTENTS

Foreword by Dan Duke

Eddie Rogers is a son in the Faith and a close personal friend. I am confident his newest book, *The Power of Impartation*, will be a tremendous encouragement to you.

I came to understand the reality of this powerful principle late in life, after more than twenty years of international ministry in hundreds of cities around the world. It was only after my first encounter with Evangelist Rodney Howard-Browne that I began to comprehend the awesome power of receiving more than a prayer or blessing, but an actual tangible impartation. That and each subsequent experience have added a whole new dimension of anointing and fruitfulness to my life and ministry, which I enjoy until today. And the same thing is available to you!

This book will open a new level of possibility and expectation in your walk of faith and supernatural ministry. It will increase your hunger for the supernatural God and His fresh touch upon your life. Anyone can pray for you. However, God appoints certain individuals to bring an impartation into your life and ministry. You will be greatly benefited by identifying those individuals who have been appointed by God to impart into your life and by developing a relationship with them.

I encourage you to read Eddie's book with an open heart and careful examination of the Holy Scriptures. In doing so, you will find a truth that has been restored to the Church of today: *The Power of Impartation.* Read and be blessed.

Dan Duke
Belo Horizonte, Brazil

INTRODUCTION

As with most projects in which the Holy Spirit is invited to be the Supervisor, things change from our original thoughts and plans. This endeavor has been no exception. Initially, my thoughts were to focus on the biblical means to receive impartation for life and ministry. Although that was accomplished, this book is not intended to be an exhaustive list of ways for the infinite God of Heaven to impart His anointing, gifting, revelation and empowerment to us so that we can do His works. As I wrote, a theme within a theme began to emerge.

A thread throughout the passages I was using seemed to unite in a common element: for the most part, what God imparted to hungry followers was received by them through other vessels of clay. The Author of impartation used men and women to transfer His blessings and favor to those who would choose to follow after their respective spiritual fathers (used generically throughout the book for both male and female), teachers and mentors.

Joshua received from Moses, Saul received from Samuel, and Timothy received from Paul. Some well known modern-day examples would be: Benny Hinn, speaking often of the influence the late Kathryn Kuhlman had upon his life, Rod Parsley acknowledging the late Dr. Lester Sumerall as his spiritual father, and Dr. Sumerall, in turn, looking back to an impartation he received from the great apostle of faith Smith Wigglesworth, in the days leading up to World War II. Could this all be merely coincidence? Or is God attempting to reveal to us a principle that was not only valid in centuries past, but will also be imperative for the completion of the last great move of God?

To my knowledge, based on extensive research into revival materials and history, I have found only one generation that extended the Kingdom of God to a greater degree than its predecessor. This was done by Solomon, who received an impartation from his father David. Unfortunately, Solomon's beginning was better than his ending.

Tucked neatly away in the last book of the Old Testament is a word that would stand through four hundred years of silence in Israel's history. Not until the emergence of *"one crying in the wilderness"* would initial execution of this prophecy be fulfilled:

Behold, I am going to send you Elijah the prophet before the coming of the great and terrible day of

the LORD. And he will restore the hearts of the fathers to their children, and the hearts of the children to their fathers, lest I come and smite the land with a curse.   Malachi 4:5-6, NAS

One man (John the Baptist), in one generation, turned a nation on its heels and prepared the way for the coming Messiah. I believe this verse is again being fulfilled today in order that we could present to the Lord an empowered Church doing His works and no longer relegating miracles, signs and wonders to the dustbin of the past. Walking in the supernatural will be an expected daily experience in the coming days.

I'm looking for a generation that will supercede the limitations of the former. I'm looking for the fulfillment of the glory of the latter house to be greater than the former. I'm looking for a greater anointing upon my sons and daughters to complete what I have lacked. I'm looking to receive a greater impartation to release to those who call me "father."

The greatest blessing I can impart to both my natural and my spiritual children is a hunger for the supernatural. I have tasted of things to come, and I cannot go back. There is an inheritance to give and an inheritance to receive. As someone once said, "God has no grandchildren." Therefore, I can only be as good a father as I am a son.

The role of spiritual fathers in the area of impartation cannot be underestimated. From the development of spiritual gifts to identifying callings and mantles, they are a gift from God to His children. While many today are seeking titles, appointments and recognition, Jesus chose to call Himself *"the Son of God,"* thus identifying with His Father. We should emphasize that in doing so, He also had the Spirit *"without measure"* (John 3:34, NLT). Isn't that the impartation we all desire today?

Come with me now as we explore *The Power of Impartation* and *The Need for Divine Appointments with Spiritual Fathers.*

Eddie Rogers
Bremen, Georgia

For though you might have ten thousand instructors in Christ, yet you do not have many fathers. 1 Corinthians 4:15

CHAPTER ONE

IMPARTATION
THROUGH ASSOCIATION

Now when they saw the boldness of Peter and John, and perceived that they were uneducated and untrained men, they marveled. And they realized that they had been with Jesus. Acts 4:13

THE MORE YOU "HANG OUT" WITH SOMEONE, THE MORE YOU BECOME LIKE THEM. IT'S AN associational relationship, and in such relationships, we often pick up mannerism, speech patterns, and even repeated words or sayings after the person we are "hanging with." This is an impartation on the human level.

How many times have you heard someone say, "You're

beginning to act (or sound) just like so-and-so"? You sound like them, even down to their opinions and ideas. You act like them, down to the way they gesture with their hands while talking. It all comes about by spending time with that person. If, on the natural level, there is this imparta-tion by association, how much more on the spiritual level?

This can be both good and bad. "Hang out" with the wrong people, and you'll get the wrong impartation—bad ideas, becoming judgmental, condemning of others, and self-righteous. (And the list could go on). "Hang out" with the right people, and you can become a better person—for-giving, patient, and gentle, etc.

> *"Hang out" with the wrong people, and you'll get the wrong impartation!*

THE LAW OF IMPARTATION IN THE BIBLE

The Bible reveals the law of impartation by association in several passages. The first I want to call your attention to is found in Exodus:

> *Then the LORD said to Moses, "Come up to Me on the mountain and be there."*   Exodus 24:12

The passage goes on to tell us that there, on the mountain, God would give Moses the law and the commandments, and this is what we most remember about it. But before there was the giving of the stone tablets, there was time for Moses to be in God's presence!

The glory of the Lord covered the mountain as a cloud for six days, and on the seventh day (seven is the number of perfection), God called Moses up into the cloud. Then, verse 18 tells us, Moses was with God on the mountain for forty days and nights. So what was he doing all that time?

Most of us consider that there must have been all kinds of information being passed between God and Moses during those days, but Exodus 25 reveals that it was not so:

Then the LORD *spoke to Moses.*   Exodus 25:1

When did God speak to Moses? Only after forty days and forty nights had already elapsed.

So what was transpiring during all of that time? I'm convinced that it was impartation by association! In God's presence, Moses was becoming like God. This is proven by the fact that when he came down the mountain, he was glowing from being in God's presence. That was a very strong and notable impartation!

Also there was a transference of the anointing that took place during that time Moses spent with God. The very Spirit, nature, and character of God was imparted into Moses' spirit.

Later, we find God asking Moses to bring seventy elders up to the mountain. God said that He would take the Spirit that was now on Moses and put it on them. Here we have another transference of the anointing.

In another chapter, we will look at Moses' servant, Joshua, and his impartation.

JESUS AND IMPARTATION

We find the same associational relationship pattern with Jesus and His disciples. Jesus *"called to Him those He Himself wanted"* (Mark 3:13), and then *"He appointed twelve, that they might be with Him"* (verse 14). Afterward, He sent them out to preach, heal the sick, and cast out demons. But clearly the priority was, first and foremost, that they simply be with Him. The more they were with Him, the more they would become like Him. This is impartation through association.

And did Jesus know what He was doing? Would just being with Him really impart something to these disciples? The Bible answers that for us. After Jesus had returned to Heaven, the members of the Sanhedrin, the ruling religious party of the day, called Peter and John to question them. What they saw was astonishing:

They realized that they had been with Jesus.

Acts 4:13

This was more than just recognizing these men as having been Jesus' disciples. Because of their boldness and power in the supernatural, they were clearly different from others. And, because of this, there was a recognition in the Spirit realm, a recognition that these men acted like Jesus, spoke like Jesus and, in fact, *were* like Jesus!

SERVING BRINGS IMPARTATION

For a number of years I was associated with a very powerful minister. The Lord spoke to me very clearly in a meeting in St. Louis, Missouri, in 1995, and told me to be a servant to him and, thus, to learn from him. During the course of the ensuing years, I spent a lot of time with this man, traveling with him around the States and even to the Philippines.

This minister operated with a very strong word of knowledge (among other gifts) and had great healing and miracle success with shoulder, neck, back, and knee injuries. As a result, we now have success in the same areas, as well as detailed words of knowledge in the area of healing. I'm convinced that it's because of impartation through my association with him.

Our relationship was based on ministerial association, but I became a servant to him, and he became a spiritual mentor to me. This same arrangement was maintained between the Old Testament prophets Elijah and Elisha. At the time of Elijah's departure, Elisha asked for a double portion of the anointing, or Spirit, that had been upon his master (see 2 Kings 2). Then he followed Elijah to Bethel, to Jericho, and down to the Jordan River, and would not leave his side until he had received his heart's desire.

Because Elisha wanted this anointing so badly, he was insistent upon going with his mentor all the way. As a result, when a whirlwind caught Elijah up to Heaven, his mantle, representative of the anointing, fell from him, and it fell onto Elisha. Elisha took up that mantle, and went forth to do great miracles. The Bible records eight miracles of Elijah, but it records sixteen miracles of Elisha.

Later, when the kings of Edom, Judah, and Israel needed to hear from a man of God, they asked for a prophet. One of the servants of the king of Israel answered and said:

"Elisha the son of Shaphat is *here, who poured water on the hands of Elijah."*   2 Kings 3:11

I find it notable that Elisha was not described as the miracle worker he was, but rather as the servant of Elijah. Those who knew Elisha recognized the power he had received through association with Elijah.

MY MENTORS

I have developed some wonderful ministerial relationships over the years, but not all of them have been for the purpose of receiving impartation. My longest lasting *impartation-through-association* relationship has been with my spiritual father, Dan Duke.

Dan adopted me as a spiritual son and has had the greatest impact upon my life of any man or woman to date. A year after the passing of my natural father, I received an impartation from Dan, first by the laying on of hands (we will discuss this in another chapter), and later in an ongoing relationship, through his wonderful advice and counsel.

My love for the nations was imparted to me while I was on a missions trip to Brazil with Dan. What I saw, what I felt, and what I heard there changed my vision for ministry forever. There is a saying, "It's better caught than taught," and that was certainly true in my case.

> *Because Elisha wanted this anointing so badly, he was insistent upon going with his mentor all the way!*

If we want to be all we can be for the Kingdom of God and do all we can do for Him, then it's imperative that we develop relationships with people who can impart to us what we don't have and also release us to impart it to others. If we're sensitive to the

Holy Spirit and follow His leading, He'll guide us to the right people, to those who can help us develop the plan and purpose He has created for our lives.

FATHER-SON RELATIONSHIPS AND IMPARTATION

I strongly believe that the most needed impartation through relationships will be those in which we become servants to our mentors, and sons and daughters to our spiritual fathers. Even now, I'm in the process of developing a relationship with a man of God who is twenty-two years my senior. He has something to impart, but not just *anything*. He has done and is doing what is in my heart to do. We must sow where we want to go.

But it's important that we allow *God* to bring the right relationships into our life. Every impartation by relation-ship I've received has been by "divine appointment." I didn't know I needed it, but God did, and He orchestrated the relationship to develop me for His greater plans and purposes. It isn't about finding God's man of power for the hour and then forcing a relationship. It's about allow-ing the Spirit of God to develop the relationship. When it's God, you'll know it.

A father-son or a servant-teacher relationship is about honesty and integrity. If you're looking for someone who will only praise you and never correct you, you don't understand what such a relationship is all about. It is about developing you, encouraging you, and supporting you, but it's also about correcting you. You must learn from your mistakes and from the mistakes of your mentor as well, for you don't want to repeat what hasn't worked in the past.

When you make mistakes (and you will), you don't need someone who will only pamper you and tell you, "There, there, everything's gonna be all right." We're training to be champions for Christ, and we can't be Christian babies, always looking for someone to give us a spiritual pacifier. Our relationship must be strong enough to stand correction, and we must be teachable enough to receive it.

Impartation is about the anointing being transmitted to you, so that you can transmit it to others. The anointing that abides *within* you can never be lost (see 1 John 2:27), but you can lose the anointing that comes *upon* you. If you do lose it, you can recover it. That's when your relationship with a mentor will become most valuable to you.

LOSS AND RECOVERY FROM LOSS

In closing this chapter, let's look at a relationship between Elisha and one of his servants:

The sons of the prophets came to Elisha to ask that they be allowed to build a dwelling place for themselves. Apparently it had become too crowded at Elisha's house. They asked the prophet to accompany them to the Jordan. There, each man would fell a tree, and they would use the logs to construct a new house for themselves.

I can picture these men working, laughing, excited about their project, each happily chopping away at his particular tree. No doubt there were comments to one another, "Why is it taking you so long?" etc., anything to keep the momentum going. Then something tragic happened.

As one of the servants drew his tool back to cut into his tree, the head of his ax flew off and dropped into the Jordan, where it quickly sank out of sight. He looked around to see if anyone else had noticed, and then panic struck his heart:

> *And he cried out and said, "Alas ... ! For it was borrowed."*   2 Kings 6:5

Anytime we lose our cutting edge, we've lost our ability to do the ministry God has called us to!

In symbolic terms, the ax head represented the anointing upon his life. It was his cutting edge. And anytime we lose our cutting edge, we've lost our ability to do the ministry God has called us to.

God can only do what He does through us by and through the anointing. Anything less than that would lower His work into the natural realm. I'm not saying that people can't be helped by natural things, but it's the cutting edge of God's power, on loan to us, that separates the natural realm from the supernatural realm.

It's the cutting edge of the anointing that lifts us into the realms of glory, to see, speak, and act on God's behalf. This is His ability, placed upon man, to do the impossible. Without it, we're helpless. Without it, we're just ordinary men. Without it, we're nothing.

WEIGHING THE OPTIONS

At this point, the young man had several options, several possible choices about what to do. For one, he could ignore what had just occurred and act like it hadn't happened. If he had made that choice, he would have been left there smiling and hacking away at the tree with nothing but a stick in his hand.

For a while, at least, no one might have noticed. Some things are not always noticeable in the beginning. After a while, though, those closest to him couldn't have helped but notice that he was whacking away at his tree, just like he had before, but now nothing was happening.

It's the same with the anointing. If you lose it, you can continue to do and say the same things as you did before, but what will be missing is the results. Pretending the loss hasn't occurred is only lying to yourself, and believing that no one else will know is only deceiving yourself.

Another option he could have chosen was to blame

the loss on someone else. "I'm in this terrible predicament because so-and-so didn't assemble this ax well enough!" Or, "Somebody must have stolen it when I wasn't looking!" It's so easy to play the blame game.

"If it wasn't for that church member ... ," "If it wasn't for that pastor ... ," "... that preacher ... ," "... that man ... ," "... that woman." "If it wasn't for that church ..."! And yet, it's no one's responsibility but our own to keep the cutting edge in our lives. Blaming other people won't change anything, and it certainly won't help you to do the most important thing—find your anointing again.

A third option available to you when you've lost your cutting edge is to simply leave and go somewhere else. When all the trees around you have fallen, and yours is the only tree standing, everyone will know that you've lost your anointing. The problem with running from it is that, even though you go to a new forest where all the trees are standing, when your brethren catch up with you, your only choice will be to move on again. So, running isn't a practical option, for it solves nothing.

And that leaves us with the only real choice we have— if we ever want to chop trees again. We have to face our failure, and be honest and truthful about it! This is where your relationship with your father/mentor will be put to the test. If you've listened wisely and obeyed the call, then he or she will be able to lovingly (without condemnation or judgment) help you find your cutting edge again.

And that's exactly what happened in the case of Elisha's servant. When he realized what had happened, he immediately went to his master, the man of God. His words, *"Alas ... , for it was borrowed,"* were spoken to none other than the prophet himself.

THE RECOGNITION OF LOSS

The first question Elisha asked the young man was, "Where did you lose it?" (*"Where did it fall?"*, 2 Kings 6:6). The servant showed him the place.

"Where did you lose it?" That's the same question the Holy Spirit will ask you, and it's an important one. If you want to experience the restoration of what was lost, you can. But before you can look for it, you have to admit that you lost it, and you have to return to the place where it was lost. This was an act of repentance, the realization that, without that ax head, any amount of swinging, even with all the strength he could muster, would have been in vain. The ax head had to be found.

Additionally, the man acknowledged that the precious tool was not really his; it was borrowed. This made the situation even more serious. He had been entrusted with something not his own, and he had lost it.

THE UTTER LACK OF CONDEMNATION

Notice that the man of God didn't condemn the younger man. He didn't send him to counseling, and he didn't say, "I told you this would happen." He didn't call the other brothers in to expose the situation and send the young man to some "time out." He didn't judge him at all for losing the ax head; he just helped him find it again. We could all learn a lesson from this.

FINDING WHAT WAS LOST IN THE RIVER

Where did the ax head fall? Into the river. Where did the servant lead the man of God? To the river. Where would his cutting edge be found? In the river!

Elisha threw a stick in the water, and the needed miracle took place. The iron rose to the surface.

I want you to notice, however, that Elisha did not retrieve the ax head for the younger man. He had to do that for himself.

Therefore he said, "Pick it up for yourself." So he reached out his hand and took it.   2 Kings 6:7

TREASURING WHAT HAS BEEN RECOVERED

If you've never lost something valuable, you probably can't imagine the comfort that finding it can bring. The fact that the ax head had been *"borrowed,"* didn't make it any less valuable. That made it more precious than ever. I can somehow see the young man clutching that piece of iron to his chest with both arms. He was holding it close, so that he wouldn't lose it again.

Because of his relationship with a spiritual father, he was now able to continue the work he had started. Some may not be able to see the importance of this whole lesson, but those of us who have walked through it can never forget the value of the impartation we have received through association.

If you don't have this kind of a relationship, ask God to bring one into your life. If you have one, then never take it lightly or for granted. This isn't about you and your ministry; it's about the Kingdom of God and passing on what you've received. You can only impart what you have. And what you've received is holy and from above. The cutting edge of God's anointing is on loan to you for the benefit of others. Treasure it accordingly.

CHAPTER TWO

IMPARTATION
THROUGH THE PROPHETIC

Then the Spirit of the LORD will come upon you,
and you will prophesy with them and be turned
into another man.   1 Samuel 10:6

REGARDLESS OF HOW YOUR IMPARTATION COMES, WITHOUT THE NECESSARY RELATIONSHIPS, it can all be in vain. The relationship to your spiritual father or mother, your teacher, or mentor is, above all, the most important thing. Many try to build relationships to get more meetings, more money, more publicity, and more recognition in the places they travel, but your relationship is about more than that.

Your relationship with a father/mentor is all about building a connection that will last you a lifetime. Even if everyone in the world recognized you and all were clamoring to have you in their pulpit, city, or nation, you still need to be responsible and accountable to someone greater than yourself.

Often, when people have no one to answer to in this realm, they can easily go off track. I realize that we all answer to God Himself, but if we ever get in a position where we're missing Him, that's when the importance of having a spiritual father/mentor comes in. Such was the case with Saul.

SAUL'S IMPARTATION FROM SAMUEL

Saul came into the Kingdom as a very humble man. He acknowledged to Samuel, the spiritual leader of the day, that his tribe was the least and that his family was the least of the least. Nevertheless, he was God's choice to become the first king over Israel.

What better position could Saul have been in? He had a relationship with a respected prophet of the day, a man of whom it was said very early in life:

> *So Samuel grew, and the LORD was with him and let none of his words fall to the ground.*
>
> 1 Samuel 3:19

Through Samuel, Saul received a prophetic word that showed that his day had come. Unfortunately, some years later, he received another prophetic word through the very same man. This time, the word was that he would lose everything he had gained.

Saul was a handsome man who stood head and shoulders above his brethren. He was also an obedient son to his father. When his father's donkeys wandered off, Saul was the son chosen to go look for them (see 1 Samuel 9). This shows that his father had learned that Saul could be trusted to carry out what was required of him.

> *Saul came into the Kingdom as a very humble man!*

When Saul and the servant who attended him could not find the donkeys, they turned to inquire of a *"seer"* (1 Samuel 9:9). That seer turned out to be the prophet of God, Samuel.

Before the prophet ever physically met Saul, God had already spoken to him regarding the young man—his calling, his position, and his anointing. Don't assume that the person God is bringing you into relationship with will know nothing about you, or about your calling, your position, or the anointing upon your life. Often, God has already spoken to them about you, sometimes even before they actually meet you. Then, when you do meet, the Spirit of God will say to them, "There he is, the man of whom I spoke to you." This is what happened to Saul.

THE POWER OF IMPARTATION

In his day, Samuel was God's spokesperson to the nation of Israel. When he prophesied, he was speaking the words of the Almighty, and, therefore, when he spoke, his words represented an *impartation* to those who would receive it. Saul received just such a word.

In great detail, Samuel described the events that would transpire before the impartation. He did this so that Saul would know, when those events took place, that he should do as the occasion demanded. It all happened just as he said it would:

> *Then the Spirit of the LORD will come upon you, and you will prophesy with them and be turned into another man. And let it be, when these signs come to you, that you do as the occasion demands; for God is with you.*   1 Samuel 10:6-7

What did Samuel mean when he said that Saul would be *"turned into another man"*? The Bible tells us that *"God gave him another heart"*:

> *So it was, when he had turned his back to go from Samuel, that God gave him another heart; and all those signs came to pass that day.*
>
> 1 Samuel 10:9

This, then, was a spiritual impartation that came through a prophetic utterance by the prophet of God, and this impartation equipped Saul to do what God had called him to do.

Saul was anointed to be king. That was his calling. But, more specifically, he was called to be king over Israel. That was his position. The Spirit of the Lord had come upon him, enabling him to do what was required of him. That was his anointing. God will never call you to do something without first equipping you with His Spirit to accomplish it.

Sadly, Saul failed, but his failure was not God's fault. He failed because he didn't take full advantage of his relationship with his spiritual father.

BEING IN THE RIGHT CALLING AND IN THE RIGHT PLACE

In your ministry, if things are not being accomplished, it could be either that you're not anointed to do it, or that it's not your calling. Also it could be your calling and yet not your position. You've heard of being in the right place at the right time? Well, you also can be in the right calling but still be in the wrong place.

If God has called you to be an evangelist, an apostle, or a prophet to the nations, but you're trying to pastor a flock and feeling frustrated, then wake up! You'll only find your peace and contentment when you're operating in both the position and place of calling and anointing God has placed upon your life.

Saul began to operate within his calling, position, and

anointing. When Nahash the Ammonite came up against Jabesh Gilead, Saul united Israel and Judah and brought about a great victory. But as he became more comfortable with his position, along with it came pride and insecurity. Pride came in because of the praises of men. They were saying what a great leader and king Saul was. Insecurity came in when those same men suddenly began to scatter before the Philistines.

> *As Saul became more comfortable with his position, along with it came pride and insecurity!*

Many, in the youth of their ministry (not necessarily their age), having received the praises and accolades of their followers, struggle with the temptation to become proud. Then, when the heat of battle comes, and those who once praised them start to scatter, they're tempted to step out of their calling and do what the occasion does not require.

Samuel was anointed and called to offer sacrifices to the Lord. When he didn't show up within the allotted time frame, Saul stepped in to "save face" and offer the sacrifice himself. He stepped out of his calling, and then had to watch as his army fled before the enemy.

What had he done wrong? The Philistines were on the

advance, and Samuel had not shown up. So what else could Saul do?

SAUL'S SAD END

Before you step out of your calling and risk losing everything, find your spiritual father/mentor and seek counsel from someone greater than yourself. Saul felt he couldn't wait any longer, yet there is no evidence that he did anything to find Samuel. He did what he was not anointed to do.

And what was the result? A prophetic word came from his spiritual father. In essence, it said, "You failed the test. Now the kingdom is stripped from you and given to another" (see 1 Samuel 13:13-14). What had been given to Saul by prophetic utterance was now stripped from him in the same way.

There's more. In this passage, Samuel declares to Saul that only his position (as king of Israel) had been taken. His kingdom would not continue, but that did not refer to his calling, that of being king. For the time being, he remained as king. This, too, would soon change.

Like Saul, I believe that many have been stripped of their position, but their calling is still intact. This is especially true under the New Covenant which declares:

> *For the gifts and the calling of God are irrevocable.*   Romans 11:29

Just because you've lost your position in one church, place, or nation, doesn't necessarily mean that God has not already ordained another pulpit, city, or nation for you. Sometimes the greatest blessings are hidden in the deepest hurts. Just because one place has rejected you doesn't mean that God doesn't have a greater place for you.

SEE THINGS FROM HEAVEN'S PERSPECTIVE

Through our natural eyes, we only see what's before us. In Saul's case, he saw his army scattering. But God can use everything as an occasion for promotion ... if we obediently follow Him and don't step out of our calling.

Could it be that God was moving those people some-where else? Have you ever considered that when things look out of control in your life, maybe God's operating on your behalf to remove the hindrances to a mighty out-pouring of His Spirit? If we're faithful in *"what is least,"* He'll promote us to *"much"*:

He who is faithful in what is least is faithful also in much; and he who is unjust in what is least is unjust also in much.　　　　　Luke 16:10

Look at things from Heaven's point of view, and re-joice that:

If God is for us, who can be against us?
　　　　　　　　　　　　　Romans 8:31

Don't allow the fear of others to discourage you. Stand in your faith and watch the Lord perform on your behalf. If everyone forsakes you, and you're left standing alone to battle for yourself, then by all means be like Shammah. He was left standing alone in a field of lentils when the Philistines attacked, but he stood his ground in that pea patch, simply because it was God's pea patch:

> *But he stationed himself in the middle of the field, defended it, and killed the Philistines. So the LORD brought about a great victory.*   2 Samuel 23:12

Don't allow the fear of others to come upon you. Don't allow the enemy to drive you away from your calling when God has told you to stay put.

FOLLOWING POPULARITY

Saul's confidence in himself and his fear of failing to be popular among the people proved to be his undoing. The battle he fought against the Amalekites was intended to annihilate them. This was because of their indiscretions against the children of Israel as they came up out of Egypt, so God specifically told Saul to destroy *"all"* the people and all their possessions. Instead, he spared their king, and he also spared the best of their flocks. When this happened, the word of the Lord came to Samuel forcefully:

I greatly regret that I have set up Saul as king, for he has turned back from following Me, and has not performed My commandments.

1 Samuel 15:10

Saul had *"turned back from following"* the Lord. So, who was he following? The obvious answer is that he was following the people for the sake of popularity.

A leader is called to lead, not to follow. When a leader bows to every whim of the people, we can know that the departure of the presence of God will follow. And the anointing will depart from that leader's life, from his position, and from his calling.

Saul's disregard for the anointing on his life and his disobedience to do what God had told him cost him everything:

Because you have rejected the word of the LORD, He also has rejected you from being king.

1 Samuel 15:23

Being king was Saul's calling, and he lost that:

But Samuel said to Saul, "I will not return with you, for you have rejected the word of the LORD, and the LORD has rejected you from being king over Israel."

1 Samuel 15:26

Being king over Israel was Saul's position, and he lost

that too. But the worst thing that happened was that Saul also lost his anointing:

> *But the Spirit of the LORD departed from Saul.*
> 1 Samuel 16:14

How sad! Saul died on a lonely hillside at the hands of his enemies, never again having experienced the presence or power of God.

WE NOW LIVE UNDER GRACE

Praise God because today we live in grace, under the New Covenant. While we can still lose the anointing that comes upon our lives, we can never lose the anointing that abides within.

The Gospel is the Good News, and the good news is, as we saw in Chapter One, *Saul's confidence in himself and his fear of failing to be popular among the people proved to be his undoing!*

that you can regain that which has been lost. Even when we fail, the enemy has no victory over us. He is under our feet because the cross spelled his defeat, and you and

I never again need experience what cost Saul his very life.

We must protect our relationships and value them. Saul didn't see the value of his relationship with Samuel until it was too late. Even then, Saul attempted to resurrect his counselor by visiting a witch, and doing, again, that which was expressly forbidden. This was a sad ending to a man who'd had such a promising beginning.

Don't Get Sidetracked

It's easy to allow things to get us sidetracked from fulfilling our calling. The enemy is good at getting us to major on minors, instead of majoring on the anointing to complete whatever is lacking in our lives. This could be lack of finances, lack of education, lack of experience, or even lack of confidence.

It appears that Timothy was both young and inexperienced, but Paul knew that the impartation the young man had received at his ordination was more than enough to accomplish what God had called him to do. God never calls you without first equipping you with more than enough to do the job. Timothy just needed to *"stir up"* his gifts:

Therefore I remind you to stir up the gift of God which is in you through the laying on of my hands. 2 Timothy 1:6

Lack isn't the only thing that can drive you off course. Believe it or not, success can become another of the minors that we often major in. It seems ironic that having a successful church or ministry could be a drawback. In the eyes of man, success is the pinnacle, and it brings the acceptance of our peers. But success can quickly turn into a prideful thing, one that obscures the greater purpose of our calling.

What *we* have done, what *we* have accomplished may keep us from the greater things God has for us. We must guard ourselves against the Saul syndrome; starting out in the Spirit and ending up in the flesh. We must stay faithful to the calling and stay close to the relationships that God has ordained.

We must stay focused. It's not just about starting the race, or even running the race well. It's about finishing the race in the grace that has been afforded us.

As long as Saul was close to his mentor, Samuel, he did well, but when distance, time, and, finally, death, separated them, Saul went drastically off course. It seems that after a successful *beginning* of ministry, the need for absolute devotion and attention from his followers became his ruin. He no longer acknowledged himself as one of the least, but rather saw himself as one of the greats.

He forgot what had brought him to that point, forgot that it was God who had chosen him, and not the other way around. Success, ultimately, was his failure.

Never allow pride in what God has done through you

to become the high point of your life. It will only lead to failure in the end. Money, fame, and the acknowledgment of your peers is never your ultimate goal. We're *in* this world, but we are not *of* it, and fame is what the system of this world seeks after.

I implore you with the words of Paul to his spiritual son Timothy:

> *Guard what was committed to your trust, avoiding the profane and idle babblings and contradictions of what is falsely called knowledge—by professing it some have strayed concerning the faith.*   1 Timothy 6:20-21

Above everything else, guard your relationships. Your calling, your position, and the anointing upon you is at stake!

CHAPTER THREE

IMPARTATION
THROUGH THE LAYING ON OF HANDS

Therefore I remind you to stir up the gift of God which is in you through the laying on of my hands. 2 Timothy 1:6

*T*HANK GOD FOR THE PEOPLE WHO HAVE IMPARTED TO US AND THEN CONTINUE A LIFETIME of ministry through us. I treasure the relationships that God has placed in my life for the eternal benefit of the Kingdom. Timothy found such a relationship in his spiritual father, Paul.

THE RELATIONSHIP BETWEEN PAUL AND TIMOTHY

The relationship between Paul and Timothy was obviously a long and enduring one. Paul encouraged Timothy in his faith by reminding him of his grandmother Lois and his mother Eunice (see 2 Timothy 1:5). Being able to call them by name and knowing of the genuineness of the faith that was in them could only have come by time spent with them.

> *Paul exhorted Timothy to "guard what was committed" to his trust!*

At the close of his first letter to Timothy, Paul exhorted him to *"guard what was committed"* to his trust (1 Timothy 6:20). This was more than a responsibility to his followers; it was the impartation which had been transmitted to him by prophetic utterance and the laying on of hands.

In the fourth chapter of that letter, Paul followed up his comments about what exactly Timothy should give his attention to (*"to reading, to exhortation, to doctrine,"* verse 13) by saying:

Do not neglect the gift that is in you, which was

given to you by prophecy with the laying on of the hands of the eldership.   1 Timothy 4:14

In other words, don't set aside the spiritual charismata, or gifting, that has equipped you to do the work. It is the Spirit that gives life!

It is the anointing that makes the difference between presenting a cold, dry doctrine and the Word of God coming alive in the hearts of the hearers. God's equipping agent is the Holy Spirit. When His flame begins to dim in our lives, our effectiveness in delivering our message, both in word and deed, dims as well.

FAN THE FLAMES

In his second letter, Paul encouragingly addressed Timothy as a *"beloved son"* (2 Timothy 1:2), and he continued to remind him:

Stir up the gift of God which is in you.
2 Timothy 1:6

This literally means, "fan the flame." When we neglect the impartation, we can become desensitized, if you will, to not depend, or, rely on, the anointing upon. The impartation enhances our sensitivity to the Holy Spirit, and gives us the keen edge on our cutting tool. Second only to the impartation to Timothy was his relationship with his spiritual father.

For those who accept that spiritual gifts were only relegated to first-generation Christians, technically speaking, Paul himself was a second-generation Christian, and Timothy, was a third-generation believer, following in the footsteps of his grandmother and mother. The Holy Spirit was still imparting spiritual gifts by the prophetic word and through the laying on of hands. And He still does it today.

THE LAYING ON OF HANDS IN THE BIBLE

There are many references to the laying on of hands in the Bible. The writer to the Hebrews even spoke of *"the doctrine of ... laying on of hands"* (Hebrews 6:2). This is probably the most familiar way the transference of the anointing occurs. For example, we have the laying on of hands for healing the sick. Jesus said:

> *And these signs will follow those who believe: ...*
> *They will lay hands on the sick, and they will*
> *recover.* Mark 16:17-18

Since the healing ministry is not the subject of this book, but rather impartation for ministry, that's where we'll continue to focus our attention.

Paul instructed Timothy not to *"lay hands on anyone hastily"* (1 Timothy 5:22). In this case, he was speaking in the context of the premature ordination of those in ministry positions in the church.

Within the denomination in which I originally grew up, we first recognized those with ministry gifts and then "set them aside" for observation. If they remained faithful to the call upon their lives, we then licensed them for ministry. It was only after a good period of time had passed and the person remained faithful and fruitful that they were considered for formal ordination. I still believe there's a lot of validity in that process. It separates those with a genuine calling from those who either have had an emotional experience or the mere choosing of an occupation.

This is not to say that the calling to ministry cannot be emotional, but when we say yes to God, we must understand that we're responding to a call:

Deep calls unto deep.   Psalm 42:7

What we're talking about here is something bigger than a professional choice. Some choose ministry because they have mercy, compassion, and a desire to help people, but that doesn't necessarily qualify them for the work of the ministry.

The first choice is God's. He said:

You did not choose Me, but I chose you and appointed you.   John 15:16

Our choice is to respond to His choosing of us. But the truth of the matter is this: When God chooses you, you

53

don't have any other choice than to respond to His grace gifting upon your life!

THE LAYING ON OF HANDS AND ORDINATION

I personally believe that with the laying on of hands at one's ordination, there comes a greater operation of the charismata (the spiritual gifts) that enhances a greater sensitivity to the anointing upon your life for the good of others.

As ministers of the Gospel, the people whom God sends into our lives are not simply there for our benefit. We have a responsibility to pour our lives into theirs, raising up still other relationships. Know that the God-ordained spiritual fathers and mentors in our lives are to qualify us to pass on our spiritual genes to children and students of our own.

This anointing must continue for the greater purpose of the Kingdom of God and not our own selfish interests. Our spiritual children should be greater in purpose, scope, and accomplishment in the realms of the Spirit than we ourselves or our own spiritual parents.

Like our natural fathers and mothers, our relationship with those who have imparted the most to us should last a lifetime. The torch should not be completely passed until our fathers/mentors have graduated from this earthly realm. Then, and only then, should our focus shift to the impartation that we pass on to others.

This is not to say that sometime, during the process, God will not bring those into our lives to whom we will begin to impart. But, for the time being at least, it is not our major focus.

We have much to receive ourselves. Through impartation, we receive the supernatural ability to operate beyond the limits of finite flesh, but there is also wisdom on a natural level that we can partake of. It is the wisdom on those who can say, "Been there! Done that!" There are invaluable lessons of experience learned by others that we can take advantage of as well.

My Earthly Father Made an Impartation to Me

In August of 1993, my earthly father went home to be with the Lord. Not only was he my natural father, but he was the first to impart into my life on a spiritual level. He held the office of a pastor for more than thirty-three

I personally believe that with the laying on of hands at one's ordination, there comes a greater operation of the charismata!

years, and it was under his ministry that I came to know the Lord as my personal Savior. This occurred one month before my tenth birthday, and it was something I never forgot or ever doubted to this day. It was a very emotional experience.

Some five or six years later, I received the Baptism in the Holy Spirit, even though our denomination didn't recognize it as a valid experience for today. It didn't seem to bother the Holy Spirit that we failed to acknowledge Him in that way.

I Met My Spiritual Father

In October of 1994, a little over a year after my father's passing, I was in a ministerial meeting in Jekyll Island, Georgia. There, I found myself standing in a line of people waiting for ministry through the laying on of hands from what most people would have called a missionary. For the sake of biblical accuracy, he was actually a "sent one," an apostle to the nations. He was Dan Duke.

As Dan laid his hands on me that day, I "went out in the Spirit" and did what many have come to call "some carpet time." (Some people doubt the validity of that experience as well, but when I got saved I became a believer, not a doubter!) Although a more commonly used term for this experience is "being slain in the Spirit," in my simple way of thinking, that sounds way too permanent. Ananias and Sapphira were slain in the Spirit, and they never got up. So I prefer to use the term "went out" in the Spirit.

As I lay there on the floor, I began to weep uncontrollably. I could feel the hand of God reaching inside of me, removing layer upon layer of hurt and disappointment from time spent in ministry with relationships that had only left me wounded. I hadn't even been aware of the fact that all that hurt was even in there. Apparently I had done a very good job of covering it up. But before God can take you to the next level, He often has to empty you of all your past. Only then can He fill you with His future.

VISITED BY AN ANGEL

After about twenty minutes of weeping out of my spirit, I became aware of an angel standing at my head. I had never had a previous awareness, or sensitivity, to such things. Now, through my spiritual eyes, a vision played itself out before me.

The angel held a pitcher of some sort in his hand. He slowly tilted the pitcher and, out of it, came a golden, honey-like substance in a continual flow. The pitcher remained in a slightly tilted position, but there was no need to increase the degree of tilt, as would be necessary in the natural, to empty something out of it. The substance flowed miraculously.

As the golden substance hit my head, I began to laugh uncontrollably. This, too, was a new experience for me. I had wept for joy and for sorrow, but this was something different. It was a gut-wrenching laughter that was, at times, so painful that I could hardly get my breath.

Then, it all stopped as suddenly as it had started, and I began to realize that something had happened on the inside of me. The hand of God had gone where the hand of man could not go. And I was now different, having been freed from the past.

> *He slowly tilted the pitcher and, out of it, came a golden, honey-like substance!*

The important thing to note here is from that moment until now, as the Holy Spirit wills, the gift of discerning of spirits has operated in my life. It came to me as an impartation through the laying on of the hands of Dan Duke.

That angel never left me. When I returned to the church where I was senior pastor, several people began to see (with their natural eyes) an angel in the pulpit with me as I ministered. They all described him in the same way. Although I have never yet seen the ministering spirits with my natural eyes, I am keenly aware of their presence.

That day, in Jekyll Island, Georgia, neither I nor Dan

Duke realized that there had been a "divine appointment" set up for father and son. While there have been others who have imparted into my life, none have taken on the kind of relationship I've enjoyed with Dan.

That wasn't the only impartation I received from him. As I related earlier in the book, my desire and call to the nations was imparted while on a ministry trip with him to Brazil in 1996. Since that time, I've ministered in other nations in South and Central America and the Pacific Rim. But, again, it's the long-lasting relationship that I value most.

RELATIONSHIPS ARE TWOFOLD

A relationship is twofold. Joshua was Moses' assistant, and wherever you found Moses, you could find Joshua. The same was true of Elijah and Elisha. Elisha did not want to leave his master's side for any reason.

When God called Moses up to the mountain to be in His glorious presence, Joshua went along:

So Moses arose with his assistant Joshua, and Moses went up to the mountain of God.

Exodus 24:13

Moses didn't go anywhere alone. When he went out to the Tabernacle of Meeting, Joshua followed him (see Exodus 33). Everyone else kept their distance, standing in the doorway of their own personal tent and worshiping God from afar.

Why did Joshua follow him and not others? It seems to me that the people made their choice, and Joshua made his. He was convinced that there was an impartation he could receive from Moses, and he was determined to follow his spiritual father until the end to receive it. Moses led Joshua to the Source, and Joshua was not about to abandon either Moses or God.

The only time we see that Moses was without Joshua was when he would return to the camp from the presence of God, and Joshua would choose to linger:

> *So the LORD spoke to Moses face to face, as a man speaks to his friend. And he would return to the camp, but his servant Joshua the son of Nun, a young man, did not depart from the tabernacle.*
>
> Exodus 33:11

Why was that? Because Joshua had come to understand that, although God uses men and women to impart to us, He is our Source, not a man or a woman. We're never the owners, just the stewards, and we must never idolize the man above the Master!

JOSHUA'S TIME HAD COME

In time, the Lord spoke clearly to Moses about Joshua's future:

Take Joshua the son of Nun with you, a man in whom is the Spirit, and lay your hand on him; set him before Eleazar the priest and before all the congregation, and inaugurate him in their sight. And you shall give some of your authority to him, that all the congregation of the children of Israel may be obedient. Numbers 27:18-20

It's important to note that the impartation is never without purpose. God never imparts to you, without the express purpose of benefiting others through you.

Is the Laying on of Hands Symbolic?

Some would argue that the laying on of hands is merely "symbolic," but when it comes to ordination and the transference of the anointing, there's nothing "symbolic" about it:

Now Joshua the son of Nun was full of the spirit of wisdom, for Moses had laid his hands on him.
Deuteronomy 34:9

For some, I suppose, the laying on of hands might be symbolic. You do have to have something before you can give something. Peter said to the lame man he and John encountered at the Beautiful Gate:

What I do have, I give you. Acts 3:6

This was true with Joshua. He went on to lead the people of Israel into their Promised Land, after Moses, his spiritual father, had passed from the scene. In this way, Joshua was able to accomplish what Moses had not been able to accomplish. And so it should be with our spiritual offspring. They should go on to do what we have not been able to do.

JOSHUA'S REPLACEMENT

When it came Joshua's turn to depart from the scene, there seemed to be no one particular person taking up the mantle he was leaving behind. At first glance, it seems that Joshua must have failed in passing his spiritual lineage to another. Why was there no spiritual son to continue where he left off?

When I noticed this, my first reaction was to condemn Joshua for his neglect as a spiritual father. Then the Holy Spirit reminded me: "Relationship is twofold."

While I'm sure there are many spiritual fathers waiting to share and impart to sons and daughters, it also requires the pursuit of the children for the wealth of their fathers. Elisha pursued Elijah, Timothy pursued Paul, and Joshua pursued Moses, but who was pursuing Joshua?

Often, immaturity and ignorance can cause us to disregard the value of a relationship. It's not just about getting an impartation. There's something more important to be learned here. When any great man or woman dies, a generation is left behind, a generation caught in a cycle of success and failure, captivity and freedom. It's God's desire that each successive generation do more and accomplish more than the last (from His perspective of the Kingdom, rather than from our own personal perspective of isolated islands of ministry). It's never two steps forward, and one step backward. His will for us today and for each successive generation is forward, ever forward!

AN IMPARTATION THAT DIES

Without sons and daughters pursuing the relationship, the impartation dies with the fathers. To whom are you accountable today? The members of a board of directors, a board of elders, or a board of deacons is not the person to whom you owe your allegiance. That person

> *My first reaction was to condemn Joshua for his neglect as a spiritual father!*

didn't call you, they didn't appoint you, and they didn't anoint you. Therefore, you're accountable first to God. He has chosen you, as He so often did men and women in days gone by, to minister His grace, prosperity, and anointing. He gives it to you through spiritual fathers and mentors He has appointed over you, and you must pass it on.

Be sensitive to the Holy Spirit, and be careful where you cast your pearls. Be wise and realize that not every person will have your best interests at heart. Many will attempt to take advantage of you. Perhaps some already have. But that will never negate the fact that God has already ordained relationships for you long before the impartation comes to pass.

Fathers, watch over those whom God has placed in your care. Children, honor and pursue those whom God has appointed over you.

CHAPTER FOUR

IMPARTATION
THROUGH GIVING
AND RECEIVING

No church shared with me concerning giving and receiving but you only.
Not that I seek the gift, but I seek the fruit that abounds to your account.

Philippians 4:15 and 17

*O*NE OF THE MOST MISUNDERSTOOD AND ABUSED PRINCIPLES IN ALL OF SCRIPTURE IS THAT of giving and receiving. At one extreme, there are those who would fight you to remain in want, believing that it's the will of God for them. At the other extreme are those who abuse this principle for their own selfish gain. There is a happy medium. Unfortunately very few who reside at these extremes will allow their opinion to be swayed, even when the truth offered comes directly from the Word of God.

With that in mind, I realize that there is the strong possibility not everyone reading this chapter will agree with it. Nevertheless, the principle of seedtime and harvest, sowing and reaping will not be altered by man's opinions or by denominational doctrine.

ABRAHAM TITHED TO SOMEONE GREATER THAN HIMSELF

Long before the Law required tithing, Abraham tithed. He was called the *"friend of God"* (James 2:23), yet he saw the need and the benefit of tithing to someone, a person, greater than himself. In Genesis 14, we find him acknowledging someone greater than himself, by giving Melchizedek (king of Salem and the priest of God Most High) a tenth of all the spoils of battle.

I would not want to debate here on these pages whether or not tithes and offerings are valid for New Testament Christianity. Our subject is impartation through giving and receiving. Rather than being controversial, let us strongly consider the possibility, as ministers of the

Word, the principle of tithing and/or giving offerings to someone greater than ourselves.

Here, I'm addressing directly those involved in the five-fold ministry: apostles, prophets, pastors, evangelists, and teachers. Personally, I am in an apostolic calling. I have sometimes called myself a reluctant apostle, simply because I'm not into titles, and I don't appreciate the abuse that often comes with the use of such titles. I believe that other ministers will recognize the particular office you're in long before you know it.

To Whom Is the Tithe Due?

For about eight years, I was the senior pastor of a growing, thriving, revival-oriented church. Within our

> *Long before the Law required tithing, Abraham tithed!*

congregation, I had a group of elders, all fivefold ministers in their own right. One of our requirements for leadership was tithing to our fellowship. (I can hear pastors applauding now, but please hold your applause for a few minutes and allow me to finish my thought. Then, you may not want to applaud me.)

One of our elders, an evangelist, had his own ministry outside our church (as well as within), and I didn't have a problem with that. In fact, I don't believe that it's a pastor's responsibility to give a platform to everyone in his church who calls themselves a minister. If you're called of God, He knows where you are and how to get you where He wants you to be. (Think of the example of Joseph.)

This particular evangelist did indeed tithe, only he tithed to his own ministry. Now, before we get all self-righteous and say (from a traveling ministry standpoint), "Well, there's nothing wrong with that," or (from a non-traveling, pastoral point of view) "That's not right. Ministers like that should tithe to the storehouse of their home church," let's first consider the pastoral office.

TITHING TO ONESELF?

Pastor, where do you tithe? I found that I was just as much at fault as my evangelist. I tithed to the church where I was the pastor. Why is that wrong? Because, in essence, I was tithing to myself. To give a true tithe or offering, one that brings an impartation, we must tithe or give offerings to someone greater than ourselves. We must tithe upward!

Please bear with me until I'm able to make my point. And remember our theme: *impartation through giving and receiving.*

How can I impart something to myself? We can only receive something we don't have. Otherwise, it isn't a true impartation.

I will never tithe to myself again. Nor will I tithe laterally into something my equal. I have many minister friends whom I consider my peers, and to them I have given and will continue to give offerings. I expect a harvest on my seed sown to them. However, I don't necessarily expect an impartation of something from someone who is my equal.

In layman's terms, if I have fifty dollars and you have fifty dollars, we're on the same playing field. If I give you a ten-dollar offering, I still expect a harvest on my seed sown, but I'm not looking for an impartation of the spiritual ability of God to take me where I've never been. Simply put, because we're on the same playing field, you can't take me where you've never been. Only a spiritual father can do that.

What is in your heart, my friend? Where do you want to be ten years from now—spiritually, financially, and ministry wise? I'm not into cliches, but this one I believe: "Sow where you want to go!"

As of this writing, I am entering twenty years of ministry. I've been an associate pastor, an evangelist (because my denomination didn't recognize apostles as being for today), and a senior pastor. For a brief period of time, I helped a pastoral peer with his church, and during that time, I was required to tithe to that church. But, as a result of tithing laterally, our finances suffered. And our ministry as well. The first week we went back on the road and tithed upward again, our finances soared, and appointments came in for ministry engagements. I'm convinced that it was because we tithed to someone greater than ourselves.

Now pastors, please don't be offended by this. I'm not suggesting that your congregation tithe to someone else other than you. When your congregation tithes to your church, they should be tithing to someone greater than themselves. Laymen, your tithes should be going to the place where you're being spiritually fed and caused to grow.

> *Giving just to get is also not a proper motivation!*

WHAT ABOUT OFFERINGS?

Now, let's discuss offerings. Anyone, fivefold ministers and laymen alike, can give offerings to ministries greater than themselves and expect not only to reap what they've sown, but also to receive an impartation from that ministry anointing. But the criteria, the motive behind all our giving should be that of a willing heart. We must never give under compulsion, out of a mere sense of duty, or out of fear of what might happen if we *don't* give.

Giving just to get is also not a proper motivation. If that's your motive, you're simply playing some spiritual lottery. Ultimately, we should give because of Who our God is, not because of what He can do for us. And we should give because our hearts are knit with His for the greater benefit of His Kingdom, not ours.

LISTEN TO THE HOLY SPIRIT

Listen to the Holy Spirit, and He will tell you when to give, what to give, and where to give. It has been my experience that most laymen, and even many preachers, already have their minds made up about what they will give in a special offering, without ever consulting with the Holy Spirit. Have you ever been in revival meetings where "love offerings" were to be received for the visiting minister, and you had your check made out long before the service began? That's what I'm referring to here.

As a side note, there's no such thing in Scripture as an "honorarium," only what we know as "free will offerings." Honorariums are man's way of compensating ministers, but offerings are God's way.

I've been in too many services where people start reaching for their set gifts before the offering is ever received, never considering the fact that the Holy Spirit may want to take them to another level through their giving. There can be a breakthrough to another spiritual plane in every area of your life by your obedient giving. God isn't limited by your set paycheck, but He is limited by your set giving. Learn to give by faith.

WHAT IT MEANS TO GIVE BY FAITH

Giving by faith is, first and foremost, doing what the Spirit says to do when He says to do it. If God tells you to

THE POWER OF IMPARTATION

do something, do it right away, before your flesh talks you out of it.

Many dear and precious people of God attempt to claim the promise of Philippians 4:19 without ever realizing that they must first qualify for that promise. They profoundly retort:

> **And my God shall supply all your need according to His riches in glory by Christ Jesus.**

How many times have you heard that quoted? Yet few stop to consider the meaning of the very first word of that verse. The *"and"* used here tells us that the promise is connected to the proceeding remarks. It hinges on verses 14 and 15 of this chapter. Those verses tell us:

> **Nevertheless you have done well that you shared in my distress. Now you Philippians know also that in the beginning of the gospel, when I departed from Macedonia, no church shared with me concerning giving and receiving but you only.**

Isn't it amazing? The great apostle Paul expected those who had given to him to also receive. People can confess and quote verse 19 until they're blue in the face, but unless they have participated in the act of giving and receiving, they're not qualified to claim the promise. If they give, they should also expect to receive, and vice versa.

What is it that you're longing for? Just to get by? Or to receive of an anointing that will break the yokes and destroy the burdens that have left you captive for so long? When I tithe or give to someone greater than myself, I'm expecting an impartation that will take me where I've never been before. I'm expecting to go to another level in every area of my life. I'm expecting God Almighty to honor His Word and bring me into a land of more than enough— more than enough anointing to raise the dead, cleanse the leper, and make the lame walk again, more than enough finances to meet all my needs, plus those of others, more than enough to fulfill all the desires and needs of this temporal world, more than enough to do what He has called me to do. That's what can happen through giving and receiving.

Our Full Responsibility

We have a greater responsibility to our spiritual fathers than to just expect spiritual blessings from them. For one thing, as their spiritual heirs, we have a responsibility (as long as they're alive on the face of this earth) to see that all their needs are met. As we are obedient to do this, we'll see the favor of God come upon us to receive the impartation, and then to bring the relationship full circle.

A full circle of impartation is what God has designed, or pre-planned. A full circle is reached when we're no longer the sons, daughters, or students. We're no longer pursuing a relationship with the father, but, rather, becoming the fathers ourselves.

The impartation of God's anointing to take you to your ultimate destiny abides within your spiritual father. If he is the father God has called him to be, then you will receive, because of your faithfulness to God and to him. Then, will your sons and daughters be able to say the same of you?

CHAPTER FIVE

IMPARTATION
THROUGH INTIMACY

But we all, with unveiled face, beholding as in a mirror the glory of the Lord, are being transformed into the same image from glory to glory, just as by the Spirit of the Lord.   2 Corinthians 3:18

HE YOUNG MAN SAT ACROSS FROM ME, EYES FIXED, HANDS FOLDED TOGETHER, AND began to speak truthfully and honestly regarding his past. He seemed to focus on some unseen object, perhaps visible in his mind's eye, as he struggled to come to grips with reality as he understood it. He admitted to three areas in his life that were out of control, and the first area was the doorway to the second and the third. I listened as he poured out his heart, thoughts that he had been suppressing for years and that had literally been eating away at his soul.

Raised in a Christian community environment, he attended "Christian" schools and colleges. Because of that, he hadn't struggled with the "usual" temptations often associated with government-run schools—drugs, underage drinking, etc. He knew the Bible and could tell its stories and quote important scriptures. There wasn't anything lacking in him that good intention could have supplied.

> *Intimacy speaks of life itself!*

Going to church had never been a struggle for this young man. After all, he had been raised in church, and old habits die hard, even when they're good habits. As he talked, everything sounded right and looked right, but something was terribly wrong. What's worse, the wrong in this young man's life had opened the door for the enemy to gain a serious foothold. Now, faced with the challenge of raising a family of his own, he had two choices. He could continue the generational cycle of being religious, while living a life that was far from ideal, "talking the talk" without really "walking the walk," or he could admit that he had a problem and seek the solution.

After listening to all of the "pros" of his religious upbringing, our attention was turned to the "cons" of his reality. His heart had come to grips with the fact that he didn't really have a personal relationship with Jesus, and he wasn't sure if he'd ever had one. Anytime he heard others speaking of intimacy with Christ, he didn't understand a word they were saying. He simply hadn't experienced it.

Intimacy with God is not a question of salvation or a personal opinion about Heaven or Hell. It's not a debate about who's saved and who's lost, nor an argument about doctrinal beliefs or denominational differences. It has nothing to do with our artificially manufactured form of Christianity, the dos and don'ts we entertain, or the list of what is approved and what is not approved by our particular tradition. Intimacy speaks of life itself!

Jesus declared:

And this is eternal life, that they may know You, the only true God, and Jesus Christ whom You have sent.   John 17:3

This word *know* is translated from the original Greek word *ginosko*. It means an experiential learning process. In this case, it means personal knowledge that produces, or leads to, a relationship (*Vine's Expository Dictionary of Biblical Words*, Thomas Nelson Inc., Nashville, TN, 1985). The tense, or mood, of this word speaks of possibility and potential. "The action described may or may not occur depending on the circumstances" (blueletterbible.org).

FACTS VERSUS EXPERIENCE

Potentially, every child of God has the ability to personally (by experience) know God. That is, to have an intimate relationship with Him. This is more than knowing *about* Him. Knowing about God, the facts of Who He is, is totally and completely different from having a personal relationship with Him.

I know about Abraham Lincoln because I've read books about him and I've watched history programs regarding him on Public Broadcasting and the History Channel. Therefore, I know a lot about what Lincoln did, and about some of the struggles he faced during this nation's horrendous war between the states.

I know, for instance, that Abraham Lincoln lost children while he was in office. I know that his wife suffered from depression, and I know how he died, who killed him, and where he was buried. Still, I never *knew* Abraham Lincoln, because I never had a personal relationship with him. Although I've read his writings, I never had the privilege of hearing his voice. And this, I'm afraid, is where many of God's children are living today. They know about God, but they've never gotten close enough to Him to actually hear His voice.

Intimacy involves speaking to one another. It involves deep emotional attachment. Intimacy is heart to heart. It is built on unconditional and unwavering love—non-judgmental, non-condemnational love.

Is it possible that one generation can have an encounter with God that changes their lives forever, and still they are somehow unable to pass that spiritual heritage on to the next generation? It isn't just possible or even probable; we have virtually succeeded in doing it in this present generation. Fortunately, here is where the value of the relationship with a spiritual father comes into play.

The young man I described has come to look to me as his spiritual father, and while it was difficult for him to discuss such personal things, it was made easier because we have developed a relationship based on unconditional love. My own spiritual father was my example in this. He showed me compassion during a very difficult season in my life. It is easy to give love when you have received love. It is a grace to show mercy when you have received mercy:

> *Thus says the LORD of hosts: "Execute true justice, Show mercy and compassion everyone to his brother."*   Zechariah 7:9

THE FATHER'S HEART

In an earlier chapter, we saw how Moses led Joshua out to the Tabernacle of Meeting, and after Moses returned to the camp, Joshua remained behind. Herein lies an important principle that is easy to miss.

Like Moses, every faithful father will always lead you to the Source of all impartation. He will acknowledge to you that there is One greater than himself. In essence, he

79

is saying, "I can only take you so far. The Greater One must increase, and I must decrease. The Greater One can give you all that I have and more. I want you to succeed beyond my potential, and to do that you must know Him intimately. You must remain with Him and let His glory change you beyond recognition." That is the heart of a father for his son.

WORSHIP MUST TAKE PLACE INDIVIDUALLY, AS WELL AS CORPORATELY

Worship is one of the greatest, if not *the* greatest, catalysts for developing intimacy with God. Being a musician has given me a great advantage that enables me to develop a worshipful, intimate atmosphere that allows the glory of God to manifest as His presence fills a room. It is in that kind of environment that we are changed *"from glory to glory."* I love corporate worship (when it is genuine), but my life has been most affected by my private times of deep communion and intimacy with God.

Many years ago, as a senior pastor, I began teaching along these lines. Most of the congregation had very strong traditional backgrounds, and worship did not always come naturally to them. At the close of my message, I asked them to begin to practice worship.

After all, you have to start somewhere. So we began to sing a familiar song together, and I encouraged the people to close their eyes, raise their hands and visualize Jesus there with them. It was a simple request.

I stood at the front and lead them by example. Then I decided to open my eyes and observe the reaction of the people. I expected to see tears, or smiles, or, at the very least, pleasant looks on everyone's faces. But I was disappointed.

No, I was more than disappointed. I was actually closer to being aggravated and frustrated. To my surprise, when I looked to see how the people were responding to my request to initiate intimacy with God, the vast majority of them, especially the older ones, were just staring back at me.

Frustrated, I tried again. This time I said it a little more loudly: "Close your eyes, and raise your hands to God!" Still, many simply stood either staring back at me or looking around at those who had complied with my request.

> *Worship is one of the greatest catalysts for developing intimacy with God!*

Now I was really troubled. What was wrong with these people? Didn't they even know what it meant to close their eyes and raise their hands?

Then I heard the Holy Spirit very clearly and gently say to me, "They cannot do in public what they've never done in private." Immediately my defensiveness vanished, and my heart went out to these people in a new and different way. They had never been taught. They didn't know God in an intimate, worshipful way, and they would have to learn.

As It Is In Heaven

Worship has a beginning, but worship will never end. It is as eternal as eternity itself.

My dear friend Ruth Ward Heflin (who has now gone on to be with the Lord) wrote in her famous book *Glory*, "Praise ... until the spirit of worship comes. Worship ... until the glory comes. Then ... stand in the glory!" (McDougal Publishing, Hagerstown, MD, 1990). Like few people I've ever met, Ruth Heflin knew God's presence. She knew the glory realm. She knew Jesus intimately. I can still hear her prophecies over me in my spirit. When she spoke, her voice carried the sound of eternity. She imparted a depth of passion and love for her Savior that few ever experience. She was a true worshiper.

Intimacy is not developed by simply being around worship, or worship services. It must become personal, and you must hunger for the presence of God more than anything else in this world. You must seek Him for who He is, not just for a ministry. When you seek Him, you will find Him, for He rewards you with Himself!

We must never equate *doing* ministry as being the same as *entering* into an intimate relationship with the Lord that positions us for impartation. Here is an example of another young man I know.

FROM RELIGION TO RELATIONSHIP

John (not his real name) was a typical high school student. He played football, liked girls, and enjoyed life in general. His classmates knew that he was a "Christian," but, in his own words, he never "pushed the envelope." His parents were well known Christian musicians and singers who traveled across the country ministering God's love in word and song. John had played drums since he was two, and now, as a teenager, he was playing with his parents in large meetings on the road.

In the mid-nineties their ministry team became the worship leaders for a very well-known and powerfully anointed evangelist. For more than five years, they traveled night after night in crusades across this country and around the world, leading people into deep realms of worship and praise before he ministered. I personally was in many of those meetings, and they were powerful.

But John's world was far more than just "church" every day. He and his family actually lived in the presence of God. He witnessed firsthand as thousands were being changed by God's power. Everyone around him was being touched and transformed—everyone, that is, except him.

It can be quite a challenge for a teenager to be able to see the world, play before thousands of people every day and still stay spiritual. John was doing all the right things for all the right reasons, but after a year or so, he came to the realization that Christianity without the power and relationship was no different than just "having some religion."

Realizing that intimacy with God was a necessity he couldn't afford to live without, he began to cry out to God. Faith is a cry of desperation that the Father always answers. This was not a generic cry for revival to touch the nations; it was a personal cry for revival: "Touch me! Change me!"

> *Intimacy with the Father, Son, and Holy Spirit should be a part of every born-again believer's life!*

There is no disappointment in God; there is only disappointment in our understanding of Him. In God's timing, on His schedule, and when John was "ready to receive," he had his encounter with God. It was in a service, just like hundreds of others he had been in before, only now he wasn't a spectator; he was a participant.

John described his encounter as being like volts of electricity, "like being plugged into an outlet." The fire of God consumed him and changed him, and he's never been the same since. Now, some ten years later, he serves as youth pastor in a church that his parents founded in Texas. He is still serving God, but now it is on a personal and very intimate level.

INTIMACY SHOULD BE THE "NORM," NOT THE EXCEPTION

Intimacy with the Father, Son, and Holy Spirit should be a part of every born-again believer's life—regardless of age or generation. Unfortunately, that just isn't the case. Many "good" people go to church all their lives and never develop a personal relationship with Jesus. For the most part, many of them don't know they can. They're unaware of the fact that God wants to personally speak to them, that it's His desire to show them His will for their lives. He wants to reveal His ways for them to walk in. He longs to prosper them, bless them and give them peace and rest. Yet, too many simply have no desire to pursue a relationship with Him.

Recently a man who is a musician on the praise team at his local church told me, "I love Jesus and all that, but I don't have the time or the hunger to pursue a relationship with Him." This was shocking coming from someone whose ministry gift is to help facilitate an atmosphere for the Spirit of God to move in. What can we expect from others?

Once even a pastor confessed to me that he wasn't personally hungry for God. So how could he lead someone into an experience he was not, himself, seeking? You cannot impart what you do not yet possess!

WHAT ARE WE COMMUNICATING BETWEEN THE PULPIT AND THE PEW?

We cannot assume these days that the people sitting in the pews of our churches are receiving everything they need, when the average weekly sermon lasts only some thirty-five minutes. The truth is that intimacy with God does not come through a sermon. From the Great Awakening of the early 1700's, from the fiery preaching of Jonathan Edwards to John Wesley and George Whitfield, Charles Finney in the 1800's, and later D.L. Moody, and on to the 1900's and Billy Graham, we have been blessed with great preaching. God has raised up men and women and used them on satellite and cable television and live internet streaming to send His Word forth to the ends of the earth. It should be clear to us that if sermons alone could change lives and bring intimacy with God, we would be the most awesome spiritual nation since King Solomon's reign.

PROFESSIONAL CHRISTIANITY vs. POSSESSIONAL CHRISTIANITY

It seems to be an obvious conclusion that in the majority of churches across America—including traditional, Pentecostal, independent, denominational, and charismatic churches—the balance between worship (true intimacy) and sermons (providing information) is grossly out of sync. Of course there are exceptions to every case, and I would never deny the positive effects of preaching with the power of the Spirit (see 1 Thessalonians 1:5). The problem seems to be that we place more importance on hearing what is said than we do on embracing intimacy with the Savior.

Without trying to sound judgmental or critical, we would have to say that we've created professionally polished pulpiteers whose job assignments are to keep everyone happy, entertained and always coming back for more. By the time the preacher appears, he hopes that the congregation has made it through the singing without losing interest, and he is now ready to present them with the main element of the service: the sermon.

The professional pastor steps onto the stage with well-rehearsed remarks that will reflect his hard work and training. The opening comments will either sound like a Shakespearian one-man play or the opening monologue from the *David Letterman Show*. From there, it will digress to a story (sometimes even a Bible story) that will have a good moral conclusion, and will end in grandiose Paul Harvey "now-you-know-the-rest-of-the-story" fashion. By the time the service is over, and the people reach the parking lot, the only thing on their minds will be their hunger. ("Feed me, Seymore, feed me!") How sad!

Again, this isn't always the case. If you are blessed to be part of a church in which the emphasis is to take everyone into the presence of God with genuine, heartfelt praise and worship, thus preparing their spirits to receive a personal message from the Bread of Life, you are blessed. The usual result is not nearly as blessed because nowhere in all of our religious rituals has room been left for the command of God's Word:

> **Draw close to God and God will draw close to you.**
>   James 4:8, NLT

This responsibility has been left to those in ministry. Whether in word or action, the laity has said to the clergy, "You are my personal high priest that stands between God and me." This tradition goes all the way back to the time of Moses:

> **Then they said to Moses, "You speak with us, and we will hear; but let not God speak with us, lest we die."**
>   Exodus 20:19

Clergymen and women have gratefully endorsed this arrangement and furthered the gap between laity and ministers—either for prestige, prominence or position (i.e. job security). In the meantime, we are supposedly reproducing spiritual offspring, but our sons and daughters don't have a personal relationship with their Father.

There is no substitute for intimacy with God—not sermons, not going to church, not taking communion, not occasionally reading our Bibles. These may all be elements that contribute to the whole, but alone they cannot replace intimate spiritual union with the Creator.

IMPARTATION THROUGH INTIMACY

TIME KEEPS ON TICKING ... TICKING ... TICKING

For those looking for a quick fix, you've already lost the battle. It won't happen in a one-hour church service or a ten-minute Bible story before bedtime. The number one enemy to developing intimacy with God is time. It takes time to develop an intimate relationship, and most of us already feel that we are pressed for it.

Let's face it, we make time for the things that are important to us. If something is a priority for you, you'll rearrange your schedule to see that it fits in somewhere. It is a very grievous thing to the Holy Spirit that we seem to have time for everyone and everything but Him.

> *There is no substitute for intimacy with God!*

"KNOCK! KNOCK!"
"WHO'S THERE?"

There have been times in our lives when the presence of God has felt overpoweringly near. In such moments, we bow our heads to give thanks for the food we're about to eat, and we nearly "fall out" because of His presence. We merely think of His goodness, and we begin to cry as we're driving our car down the road. In these moments, everything we touch, hear or see seems to carry the fragrant aroma of His presence. He is knocking at our door. He said:

> *Behold, I stand at the door and knock. If anyone hears My voice and opens the door, I will come in to him and dine with him, and he with Me.*
>
> Revelation 3:20

The Greek word here translated as *dine* (*sup* in the KJV), means to share the principle meal of the day. This was a time at the close of the day when a family would gather together and share, not only their evening meal, but also their day. It was a time of intimacy, of listening and being listened to, a time of communion and fellowship. With us, these are the times when the door of our heart is open and constant spiritual union is taking place.

And that's great, but what about the times when God's presence seems very far away? Is there anything we can do on our end to change things? Why would He be so close one day and so far away the next?

FATHER KNOWS BEST

The best way to illustrate this would be to consider a toddler learning to walk. Their steps are quite precarious and awkward. The problem isn't usually taking a step; it's getting the steps to come consistently, one after the other. When it happens, a father will hold out his arms to get his child to come to him.

Then, as the child takes a step toward the father, the father takes a step back. Why? To get the child to continue his pursuit and to develop his strength and skills. Finally, there is the reward of being caught! In the same way, God *"is a rewarder of those who diligently seek Him"*:

> *But without faith it is impossible to please Him, for he who comes to God must believe that He is, and that He is a rewarder of those who diligently seek Him.*   Hebrews 11:6

Persistent knocking always brings results.

I'M GONNA KNOCK ON YOUR DOOR

And He said to them, "Which of you shall have a friend, and go to him at midnight and say to him, 'Friend, lend me three loaves; for a friend of mine has come to me on his journey, and I have nothing to set before him'; and he will answer from within and say, 'Do not trouble me; the door is now shut, and my children are with me in bed; I cannot rise and give to you'? I say to you, though he will not rise and give to him because he is his friend, yet because of his persistence he will rise and give him as many as he needs. "So I say to you, ask, and it will be given to you; seek, and you will find; knock, and it will be opened to you. For everyone who asks receives, and he who seeks finds, and to him who knocks it will be opened."   Luke 11:5-10

Just as a father knows what is best for his child, so our heavenly Father knows what is best for our personal spiritual development. If we are to pursue spiritual intimacy, there will, of necessity, be times when we will have to do the knocking. That is part of the pursuit. The reward comes the moment He opens the door!

When you humble yourself before God, you are preparing your heart for a visitation from Heaven!

The man who went to his friend at midnight didn't get what he requested because of their friendship. He got it because of his persistence. He refused to be denied. That kind of faith requires something more of you than to say to God, "I'll try to work You in."

We've all been dealt a *"measure of faith"* (Romans 12:3). When you humble yourself before God, you are preparing your heart for a visitation from Heaven. Humility is faith recognizing your absolute dependence upon God for everything—including those intimate times.

For thus says the High and Lofty One
Who inhabits eternity, whose name is Holy:
"I dwell in the high and holy place,
With him who has a contrite and humble spirit,
To revive the spirit of the humble,
And to revive the heart of the contrite ones."

Isaiah 57:15

DON'T KISS AND TELL

We have probably all quoted Jesus at some point, when He said:

Do not ... cast your pearls before swine.

Matthew 7:6

Sometimes intimacy requires that we keep those pearls—swine or no swine. There is an intimacy between a husband and a wife that should remain between them only. Equally so, the Father desires intimacy with us, and He desires to impart revelation to us that will remain with us. Paul said it this way:

But I do know that I was caught up into paradise
and heard things so astounding that they cannot
be told.   2 Corinthians 12:4, NLT

He is declaring, "There is an intimacy I wish I could tell you about, but I can't. It's too personal." Can you

93

imagine having times of spiritual intimacy with God that are so awesome you just can't tell anyone about it? That's what He wants for each of us.

And it's there waiting for us. God isn't a respecter of persons. He desires intimacy on that same personal level with each individual. This isn't about having an encounter with God so that you can sell more books and tapes and get more preaching appointments. This is about desire. It's about living, loving, and adoring the Lover of my soul.

WORSHIPING HIM COMES BEFORE WORKING FOR HIM

Martha was busy working for Jesus, but Mary found the *"good part,"* sitting at His feet (Luke 10:42). Our busyness for Jesus is only as good as is our time sitting at His feet in adoration and praise. Effective ministry *for* Him is a direct result of affectionate ministry *to* Him:

> **As they ministered to the Lord and fasted, the Holy Spirit said, ...**   Acts 13:2

God speaks to us in times of worship, and worship takes place in the heart, not in a sanctuary. Jesus said that the Father is seeking those who will worship Him *"in spirit and truth"* (John 4:23). Worship is just another aspect of intimacy, whereby we are embraced by the One with whom we desire communion.

According to this promise, when we engage in true worship, either alone or corporately, the Father comes looking for us! The New Living Translation says it this way:

> *But the time is coming and is already here when true worshipers will worship the Father in spirit and in truth. The Father is looking for anyone who will worship him that way.*
>
> John 4:22-23, NLT

RSVP REQUIRED

An invitation for intimacy has been issued. The Eternal God, Savior, and Creator of the universe desires time with you. When it seems that He is not standing at our door knocking, He has provided ways for us to seek Him out. Let's review how we can position ourselves for impartation, the likes of which will open Heaven and open our hearts for visitations of an other-worldly kind:

HUMBLE YOURSELF:
> *If My people who are called by My name will humble themselves, and pray and seek My face, and turn from their wicked ways, then I will hear from heaven, and will forgive their sin and heal their land.* 2 Chronicles 7:14

BE PERSISTENT:

Keep on asking for something to be given, and it shall be given you. Keep on seeking and you shall find. Keep on reverently knocking, and it shall be opened to you. For everyone who keeps on asking for something to be given, keeps on receiving, and he that keeps on seeking, keeps on finding, and to the one who keeps on reverently knocking, it shall be opened. Luke 11:9-10, KSW

LEARN TO WORSHIP EFFECTIVELY:

You see, the Father too is actively seeking such people to worship him. John 4:23, NCV

WHO DO YOU KNOW?

What we do for the Kingdom and the impact it will have on eternity all comes down to one thing—the level of intimacy we enjoy with God. Daniel prophetically spoke about a people who would know Him intimately.

But the people who know their God shall be strong, and carry out great exploits. Daniel 11:32

Hebrew grammar scholar and professor, Wilhelm Gesenius (1786-1842), spoke of the phrase *"who know their God"* as meaning: "to perceive, to come to the knowledge of, by seeing, by hearing, and by experience" (New Wilson's Old Testament Word Studies, by William Wilson, Kregel Publications, Grand Rapids, MI, 1987.). Knowing God intimately is a matter of desire and choice. In the business world, it has been said, "It's all in who you know." And so it is in the Kingdom of God as well.

A PROPHECY

There are divinely orchestrated appointments at hand where the destiny of individual lives will be influenced and forever changed. The fate of cities, regions and nations are about to be severely impacted by an army of believers who have stormed the gates of Heaven with prayer, fasting and righteousness. They've gone before the throne of God and taken hold of the power of the Almighty.

An anointing of epic proportions has been imparted to a generation that will invade the territories of principalities and powers, to render them impotent before the King of Kings, to whom their allegiance is given. A tsunami wave of the

> *What we do for the Kingdom all comes down to one thing — the level of intimacy we enjoy with God!*

glory of God will precede them, to set at liberty the captives of religion. This super anointing will trample sickness and disease and will leave life where death formerly prevailed.

Angels will be released in greater number and be seen to fight alongside these warriors from another realm. Eternity has invaded their soul. They have become a prisoner of God's love, and nothing on earth will stop their glorious crusade or triumph over them.

They will walk the path of mercy and truth, for they have received, from the Father, an impartation with no limitations. They have been given the ability from Heaven to make His enemies His footstool. The Captain of the Lord's host is their Commander, and their mission will not fail.

A FINAL WORD

It's time to make the connection. It's time for fathers to find their sons, and sons to find their fathers. The "hookup" is done by the Holy Spirit.

If you've already found your father, it's time to honor him as never before. If you've found your sons and daughters, its time to impart to them and then release them into the harvest.

If you have yet to make this divine appointment, it's time to ask the Father of all fathers to set up your encounter. He has reserved for you a date that you will never forget. Don't be late.

For though you might have ten thousand instructors in Christ, yet you do not have many fathers.   1 Corinthians 4:15

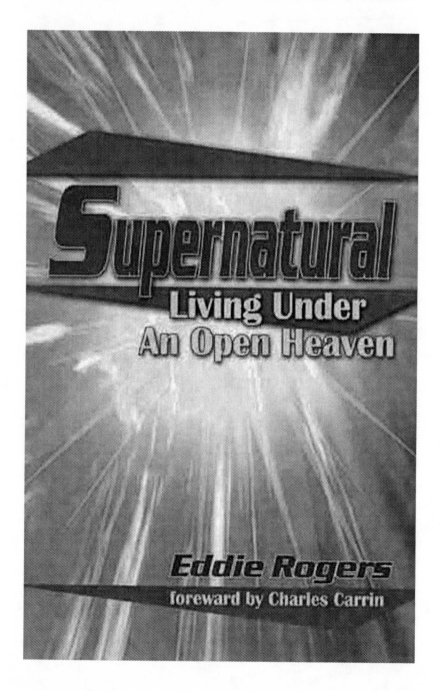

Supernatural
Living Under
An Open Heaven

Eddie Rogers
foreward by Charles Carrin

MINISTRY CONTACT INFORMATION

Revival in Power
Eddie and Michelle Rogers

Visit us on the World Wide Web for contact information, updates, new products, and devotionals at:

www.revivalinpower.com

LaVergne, TN USA
05 September 2009
157107LV00002B/11/A